Word

Mark Gwynne Jones

Thomas
Best
Wordwishes
M. G. J
2017

route™

First published by Route in 2014
PO Box 167, Pontefract, WF8 4WW
info@route-online.com
www.route-online.com

ISBN : 978-1901927-64-1

Editor: Ian Daley

Cover Illustration and Design: © Helen Brownsword

Book Illustration and Design: © Helen Brownsword

With special thanks to: Stephen Parkes for planting the Wordworm; Arthur for the princely cat; Sam for the laser guided bomb and most of all Louise.

Hats off too, to the students of Springwell Community College and their Curriculum Leader for English, Nerys McCabe; and the pupils of Shirland Primary and their teacher Fiona Banks: for all their support and invaluable help in selecting the poems.

Acknowledgements are also due to the students of Becket, Retford Oaks, Sutton Centre and Christ the King, Nottinghamshire for wondering aloud: *If I Were a Poet...*

Some of these poems were written with the support of a writing bursary awarded by the Arts Council of England.

Printed and bound by CPI Group (UK) Ltd, Croydon, CR0 4YY

For Sam and Arthur

Contents

Wordworms! (Part 1)

Words will sleep in the pages of books
entranced inside a nest of leaves.
They'll sleep, sometimes, for hundreds of years
waiting for you
to mouth and breathe their names.

Like grubs that sleep, dreaming of wings,
they curl up like the chrysalids
until one day a sudden breeze
ruffles their nest… utters their names…
          and muttering, spluttering out they slip…

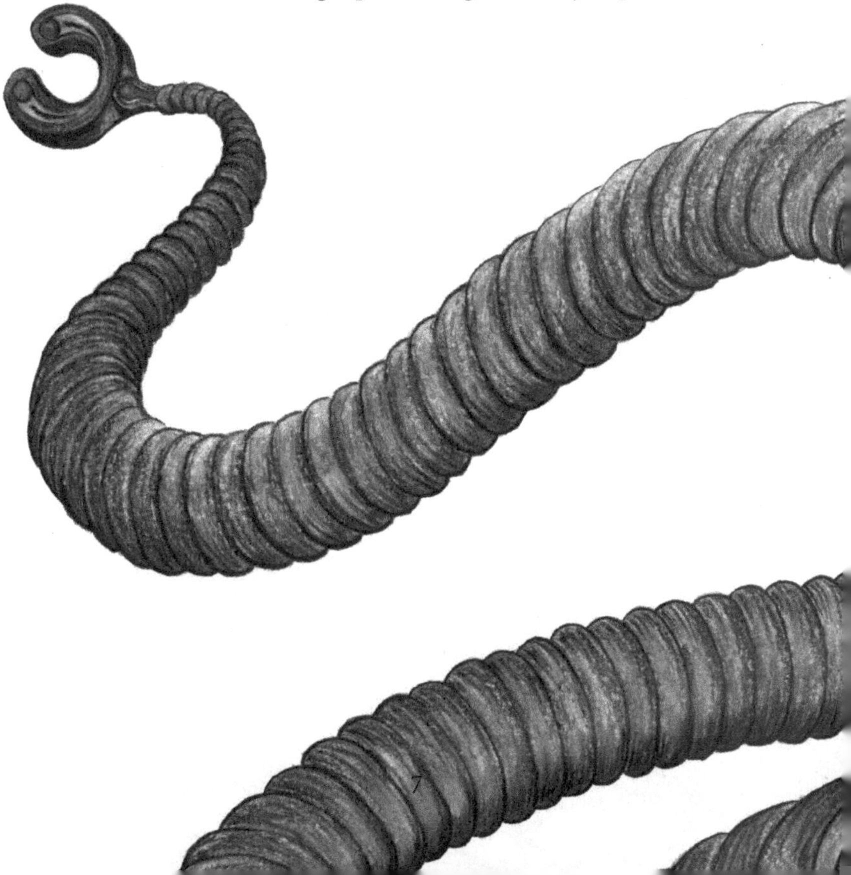

Words... They're Alive!

My God they're alive...
The sounds we shape to speak our minds
have hatched like larvae
covered in fur
slept in thought
to wake as words
with wings...
And now, we watch them
flutter and sing:
of dragonflies, aeroplanes, wasps and bees
of sweetness and lies and the restless breeze...
They're alive!
The sounds we shape to speak our minds
speak our minds:
say how you'll feel
say what's real
and sometimes lie about what we are:
Me?... I'm as stupid as an empty jar
of butterflies...
or rats with eyes!
Or mice with wings escaping to squeal
and flutter about with how I feel...
Their bodies are made of sound and sense
and their wings are as fine as the present tense
that's as real as... well, what is real
when words are alive?

If I Were a Poet...

(Lines written with students of Becket, Retford Oaks, Sutton Centre and Christ the King, Nottinghamshire.)

If I were a poet…
I'd grow some wings
fly to the moon
then bring it back and give it to you!

If I were a poet…
could I erase
the mistakes I've made?

If I were a poet…
could I bring someone back?
Someone I'd lost.

If I were a poet…
I'd photocopy myself
and send my copy to school.

If I were a poet…
I'd understand the language of birds
talk to animals and eat clouds.

If I were a poet…
I'd answer unknown questions.

If I were a poet…
I'd be the most handsome teen ever.
But hey, that's already true.

If I were a poet…
I'd turn celebrities
into thin air
then sell them on eBay,
in a jam jar!

If were a poet…
I'd know just the right words
to make you fall in love…

I Fancied This Girl...

When I was young
I fancied this girl in the year below,
taller than me, blonde and with a slightly stuck up nose.
I fancied this girl in the year below
but did she fancy me I wanted to know
and how could I tell her what my feelings were
and get her to like me the way I liked her.

I fancied this girl in the year below
and so, I decided to give her a Yorkie Bar.
My favourite chocolate – chunky and hard.
In fact, I liked Yorkies that much that...
I decided to give her some of my mum's cooking chocolate
carefully wrapped in the Yorkie Bar wrapper.
I didn't attack her.
I said *Here's something I thought you might like...*

I fancied this girl in the year below,
taller than me, blonde and with a slightly stuck up nose
but did she fancy me I wanted to know
and how could I tell her what my feelings were
and get her to like me the way I liked her.
So, I hid her bag and hummed her favourite song,
I stood in her way, I stuck out my tongue,
I trod on her toes, I called her names
Look up her nose!
I exclaimed,

but nothing seemed to work.

One Particular Lamppost

You might not know it but lamppost D6359 is alive.
Hit by a car he leans to the left
and hums to himself during the night as he has no friends
except for lamppost D6358,
but that one's faulty.

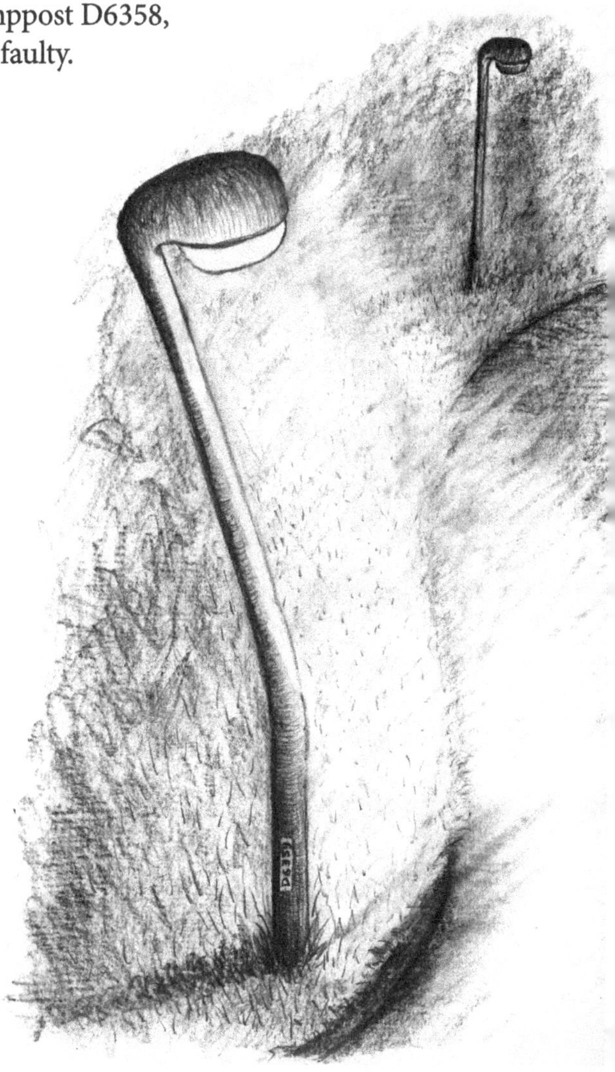

Tell Her I Love Her

Tell her I love her a lot. No,
you better not tell her that.
Just tell her I fancy her.
Tell her I think I fancy her quite a bit.
Tell her I think I fancy her quite a bit more
than I thought I fancied her once before.
Tell her 'he's not asking you out… but if he did…'
No, don't tell her that.
Just tell her I like her
a little.
When I say a little I mean
tell her 'he thinks you're alright'
tell her 'he thinks you're not bad'
tell her… O forget it I'll tell her
I bloomin' hate you!

No! Go to Sleep... said the Lazy Moon

Give us a kiss…
mouths a fish
where the water slips

Give us a snog…
bellows a frog
from a floating log

Let's have a hug…
sighs a slug
in his search for love

No! Go to sleep… said the lazy moon

I'll be your dog…
barks a fox
alone in the fog

Just rub my back…
whispers a bat
with an itchy back

Let's have a hug…
sighs a slug
in his search for love

No! Go to sleep… said the lazy moon

Give us a snog…
bellows a frog
from a floa… *Oh, go on then!* said the moon

And the magic began…

I'll Be Bird, You Be Tree...

(If you never leave me… I'll never leave you. Not now, not ever.
'Fundevogel' **The Brothers Grimm***)*

I'll be water, you be roots
I'll be the wasp, you be the fruit
I'll be bird, you be tree
and they'll never know – it's you and me

Yes, I'll be branches, roots and leaf
and you be feathers, fur and beak
tell me all that you can see
and they'll never know – it's you and me

And if they ask where we've gone
or come looking with their guns
we'll sing,
how we'll sing

And if they stop, point to tracks
say *they were here* looking back
we'll sing,
how we'll sing

I'll be moonlight, you be shadow
walking with them over the meadow
I'll be rustling, you be the breeze
and they'll never know – it's you and me

And then at church, evening prayer
whispering to God, condensing air
I'll be Devil, you be Lord
and they'll never know – we're in both words

And if the woodman tries to climb us
sharpening his axe to split and find us
we'll sing,
how we'll sing

And if the cook comes to spoil us
lights a fire on which to boil us
we'll sing,
how we'll sing

I'll be the sun, you be the road
I'll light the way, you bear the load
burning heads, bruising feet
and they'll never know – it's you and me

I Wish I Didn't Have to Go to School...

I wish I was a bejewelled fish
a red and golden trout,
in a flash, unseen, I'd dart upstream
you would not catch me out!

I wish I was a princely cat
panther black,
alive to nature's laws,
in a silent pounce I'd catch that mouse
then lie and lick my paws.

I wish I was a lazy cow
just lying there, chewing the cud.
Though people'd shout *You... lazy cow!*
I would not change or budge.

All nature's things know how to be;
the fish, the cat, the cow,
each one knows instinctively
the what, and why, and how.

They don't need to go to school:
the fish, the cat, the cow,
they've not forgotten who they are
or what, or why, or how.

Caution: Remember to Breathe

Warning: Pencil Case.
This pencil case may contain sharp objects such as pencils.

Danger: Puddle 3.6cm Deep!
Anyone lying face down in this puddle is liable to drown.

Attention: Do not eat pebbles.

Will you – won't you – do you – don't you?
He couldn't quite decide
whether to try and concentrate
or let the lesson slide,
whether to staple his tongue to the desk
or quietly bite his lip.
The pictures flashing through his head
were that, the other and this…

Shall I – shan't I – can I – can't I
that, the other and this.
At break they're trying to
break my bones
and put me in the ditch.
Should I try to put up a fight
or squeal and grass them up?
My uncle says we've all been bullied
it's the thing that makes us tough.

Do I lack it? Can I hack it?
The thing that makes us tough.
I tried to find it in the packet
of cigarettes I chuffed.
I was smoking on the cross country run
in clouds of hide and seek
with the boys who think it's big, somehow,
to make their bodies weak.

Will he – nilly – nill he – willy
make his body weak?
Perhaps the girls will notice me
if I show them I can take
more poison than the next boy.
Here, where's that lighter fuel?
If I drink some, right, then ask for a light
they're bound to think I'm cool.

Could you – would you – would you – could you
ever think I'm cool?
Should I think for myself
or listen to these fools?
Should I staple *their* tongues to the desk,
or quietly bite my lip?
The pictures flashing through his head
were that, the other and this.

Recycling Tanks

(Let's be careful how we dream)

Imagine a school where all the bullies
were rounded up and cooked in curry.
Or, a battlefield where all the tanks
were taken to recycling banks
and turned into the pots and pans
to feed the poor in desert lands.

Imagine a school
where the most frightening teacher
was shrunk to the size of a centimetre
and what was once a booming voice
became the squeak of a little mouse!

But surely, such a world and such a time
can only exist inside the mind?

No. Telephones and aeroplanes
were but a dream in someone's brain.
So, sometimes our imaginings
have the life of living things...

O please, please, please
let's be careful
how we dream.

Fingereye

The boy with the eye on his index finger
could peep round corners
and over walls,
look inside peoples' pockets
and underneath their doors,

he could see behind his back
and watch those watching him,
keep one eye on the shuffling pack
and choose which hand to win,

he could see how others see him
so never needed mirrors
to check his hair, look up his nose
or even down his ears,

he could copy his classmate's work
whilst staring into space,
the boy with the eye on his index finger
and two upon his face.

In human biology with Mr Boffin
the boy would sit enrapt
reading J.R.R. Tolkien
closed upon his lap.

So, while the class was studying
how an eye is but a lens,
he saw the whole of middle earth,
the mountains, fire and plains.

When not in use he kept it shut
hidden by a wink,
in case when others saw it
they'd scream and call him freak!

Or run to tell the teacher
who'd sell him to the fair:
The boy with an Eye on his Index Finger!
Step right over here...

But ogling was his pastime.
Ogling was his love,
and secretly he ogled
as often as he could.

Till once when he was ogling
beneath the staffroom door
Mrs Botham saw the eye
and pinned it to the floor.

Thomas Mole!? You monstrous boy!
Just what is on your hand?
She didn't sell him to the fayre
but to those who'd understand:

the doctors at Great Ormond Street,
conferring in a hum:
The boy has an eye on his index finger...
I suggest we keep this shtum!

They came to cut and strip some cells
Umm... just to do some tests
then from those cells they tried to grow
a fingereye themselves.

A cloud, a blob
            ...a purple rod
a furry sausage roll
in fluid grew from something blue
into a perfect clone!

They cloned it once.
They cloned it twice.
They cloned a thousand eyes
each on the end of an index finger
blinking at the skies.

The World is at Your Fingertips
the headlines did proclaim
and everybody wanted one
those eyes are all the rage.

So, be careful on the corridors,
beware upon the loo,
for a boy with an eye on his index finger
might be watching you!

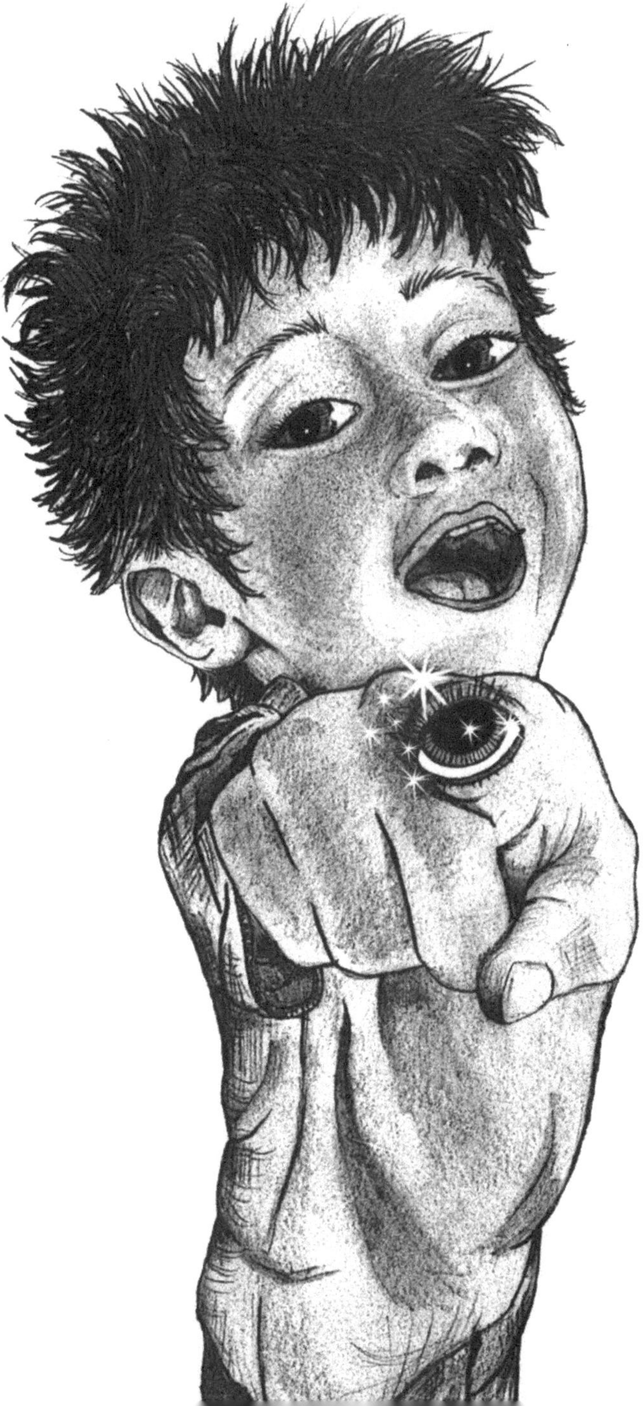

The Art of Eating Aeroplanes

The Japanese man who ate a plane.
Did he have to train?
Was it in the nuts and baltis?
Probably not; he was from Japan.

But closer to home,
if that was the yin then this is the yang:
a guy at the local sewage works
rebuilt it, piece by piece,
and now runs sight-seeing flights over Mount Fuji!

Look! Man eating aeroplane.
No… aeroplane eating man!

The Suicidal Swans of Swaffham

If you've ever wondered how a swan can break a man's arm, then here's how: *The Suicidal Swans of Swaffham* are trained to dive bomb their targets and can break a man's arm from an altitude of 300 feet or more. Though less expensive than a laser guided bomb or G45 Drone, *The Suicidal Swans of Swaffham* can, at anytime, break any man's arm anywhere on the planet and will even operate in such treacherous places as France, Germany, Italy and Spain. With some pride I am now able to report a wedge of Her Majesty's Swans was recently sent to defend the Rock of Gibraltar – a place as British as they come.

The Trumpeter and Whooper Swans sing as they start to dive, a swansong as the dive bomb invariably kills them. The Mute on the other hand offers no such warning and falls instead as silently as a breeze-block painted white. It is hard to say which is more surprising, as men who have just had their arms broken by the full force of a 33lb swan falling from the sky are usually rendered speechless. Their silence preserves the secrecy of one of our greatest assets in the war on terror – *The Suicidal Swans of Swaffham.*

Hopes are high as the swans leave our shores and are given a fond farewell by well wishers gathered on the White Cliffs of Dover.

Rats!

There's rats in the cellar.
I tried to get them out
by hurling abuse and a bottle of stout
that smashed on the steps of the cellar stair.
I was watching the tail of a rat disappear.

So I tried to be clever
I tried to be kind
with a trail of sugar to the door outside.
The following day none could be found,
I was Pied Piper of Matlock Town!

And then that night, happily to bed,
under the covers I rightfully said:
Rats?! Oh, Sugar! Sugar? Rats!
The place was just a heaving mass
of Rats Sugar Sugar Rats
I was the candy-man for the big eyed rat.

From down in the cellar
up the hall
they follow me to bed when the shadows fall
and fill my mind with devilish dreams,
lurid acts and ugly scenes.

There's rats in the cellar.
I've got to get them out.
I hear them at noon
when there's no-one about.
They've scratched my scruples,
ripped my clothes.

I thought I might try an overdose
of the purple pellets of vermin poison.
Well, *Ratus Norvegicus* seem to like them.
It makes them big,
it makes them strong.
They chased me naked round the lawn.

From behind lace curtains watch
the neighbourhood of Cuthbert's Lodge
and the following day the doorbell rang;
it was the public health and safety man.
I understand th'as got Rats! he said,
without a smile.
I shook my head for quite a while,
as he proceeded to recite with a tireless tongue
Health and Safety – Act I.

By the end of Act II, I could comprehend
that this man meant our lease would end
unless I could prove beyond reasonable doubt
that all of the rats had been taken out.

His words they rang like a peal of bells
from glittering towers of principles.
A ceaseless echo throughout the day,
his words were jangling nerves at play:

O their whiskers twitch
and their eyes are bright,
bulging with a demon-light.
From out the sewer they come in droves
to live like freaks in a human home.
In perfect coils their heavy tail

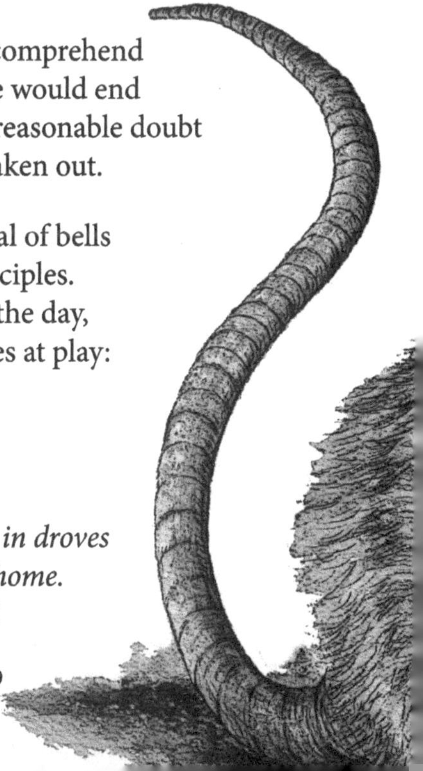

drags behind like a lady's trail.
Their teeth are keen, so too their claws!
Watch them glide across the floor.

All night long I walked the boards,
waiting for the rats, of course.
With a bottle of stout and a fine long knife
I was wearing a wig to perfect a disguise.

O their whiskers twitch
and their eyes are bright
bulging with a demon light
carried from the dark of sewerage drains
to burn like mad in human brains!

Dressed like a typical farmer's wife
I was cutting off tails with a carving knife.
Did ever you see such a thing in your life?

Rats!? Naa mate, not here, no…
I've got some guinea pigs though!

What Do You Think?

Think fast
think things
think faster than wings of light and sound,
how fast do your thoughts
leap and bound?
On what legs, or wings, or slippery fins
do they run or fly or sink and swim?

Think near, think far
think of the star
that gives us light inside this jar of blue,
inside the word, inside your head
a star both old and new;
does it live in the world, the word or inside you?

What do you think?

You can't stop thinking!
Really?

Then don't think of an apple...

Don't think of its type
don't think of its colour, or if it tastes very nice.
Don't think of the wasp… that's burrowed inside
with sticky veined wings
and yellow black stripes
glistening round
its waspie
body
that won't end in a sting
so long as you don't
think of an apple.

See. It's true.
These are just words
but I bet you see them inside of you.

What do you think?

Ick Bic Biro Stick

Ick Bic Biro Stick
draw a map and make it quick!
I need to see just where I am…
said the lost boy to the magic pen.

But the magic pen had a mind of its own
and sure it could draw a map if it chose
but instead it doodled and doodling drew
…a goose in a bottle and shaded it blue!

Sic Bic Biro Stick!
That's not a map and I've no time for tricks.
The light was fading, he was far from home
and something was moving close by the road.

Ick Bic Biro Stick!
Draw a map and make it quick!
At least show me which way to run…
said the lost boy to the magic pen.

So, as magic pens are able to do,
it guided his hand and carefully drew
the outline of the darkening hills,
the lane homewards running through fields,
the steep sided valley,
the railway lines,
the place where he found his brother's knife,
his old school, the lamppost that leans,
the flowerpot hiding the front door key…
Yes, Ick Bic Biro Stick!
But which way!?

At this the pen paused,
as if waiting, listening…

and then, with a final flourish
disguised the map as a Mistle Thrush
singing above the Railway's End
where, suddenly the boy could hear one sing:

„Come follow me... Come follow me…"

Ick Bic Biro Stick
Your ink is the blood
of creatures with wings!

The Giant Toad

(A poem for when you're worried about the future)

When the future squats
like a giant toad
hunched in darkness
          at the top of the road,
croaking bubbles of worrisome thought
that burst in shadows where you walk

don't take a stick with which to beat him off
or, throw a spear to puncture his heart,
his heart is made of hopeful dreams
                    and foolish fancy,
your weapons would only make him angry.

And, remember who you're trying to kill.
Would you wish your future ill?

No. Instead, gently amble to his side
and sing to him, to his golden eyes.
Sing of water lilies, the scented shores
and offer him balm for his warts and sores,
and plant a kiss upon his fevered brow…
and behold… the future is here…
the toad is now.

The Future

It's Only Water...

Rain, rain, beautiful rain
why do they hate you so?
With cagoules and drains and glass double-glazed
they try to stem the flow!

Rain. Bountiful rain.
The cause of creation to grow
from an earthen corpse to creatures that walk,
why do they hate you so?

From the window bay
of a block of flats
in which I live upstairs
I saw the city awake
in a gorgeous lake
awash with people, dogs and chairs.

From far above
I said: *Let go!*
It's only water after all!
but to the telegraph wire
clung a mother and child
perfectly parallel above the floor…

The water was rising,
the drains were blocked,
cars like boats were sailing away.
I tried to tell them:
It's only water!
but: *Bog off y' glug… glug… glug… glug…*
was all they could say.

In the blackness above us
the heavens are holy,
as holey as a culinary sieve.
I tried to show them
it's only water
by lapping it up in a plastic lid.

I said: *Let go!*
Me telegraph wire's gonna' snap
with all your weight!
but like clothes in the wind
on the washing line,
they hung outstretched in the rushing spate.

I chucked them ducks.
I lobbed them loofahs.
I sent them bars of soap.
But every time their faces rose
above the surging water floes
all I heard was: *Rope!... Rope!...*

I said: *Come on! It's only water –*
pretend you're in the bath!
but the Amateur Dramatics Society
were getting carried away,
and none of them laughed.

O as pretty as the city of Venice – she was
marooned in the morning light,
suffused in a surge of water
purging the town – not of life
but of all those – who live in bungalows
and never wanted to know me
until they needed help!

What Weather Next?

Blow
ing
holes
in radio
schedules
voices call you *Severe*
but you're a – wet wind,
wild and mild and somehow
more unsettling. During the night
our front door could barely keep you out.
Your shrieks and howls laid siege to the house. *Wild…*
yes, but words like *Severe…* feel premature.
Your screaming is more like
a warm blooded spirit…
fleeing. Desperately
searching for
some
where
to
hide
!

The question is… from what?

Cats Across the River...

I've got to get across that river of steel
I'm looking for a space
looking out for the can't be late... can't be late... can't be late... race
I'm standing, waiting, looking for a space
but the cars keep coming
to slap my face
look right... look left... look
there isn't a break, there isn't a gap
there isn't room to swing a cat
in fact, there isn't a cat to swing
I know that, 'cos I've seen them flat on the hot tarmac
and right now, picking one up wouldn't be easy...

Rubbish!

A Cheese and Onion Blue
fluttering through the car window…
A Coca Cola Red under your legs…
M&M's Yellow from a little fellow,
they fly and flap about…

A plague of ridiculous parrots!

Rustling and crackling how their cackling
jeers at the primroses
All tucked up in their tidy beds!

Hustling and hassling how their prattling
sneers at senior citizens:
That's right, we are rubbish…
And what are you so good at? eh? eh?
What are you so bloomin' good at!?

Shhh…
If you listen
you can hear them…
breeding under the bushes
and all the while
fearing the man… with the grabber!

Nervously they gather
in corners… in lay-bys… in the eddies of streams…

Misfits
          meeting
in the park
trembling like drunks… without a drink.
Their blotched and garish faces
an offence to those who made
and rejected them
so soon.

Yeah, we are rubbish… and proud of it!

Plasticman

I knew a man
who lived within
a disposable plastic Sainsbury's bin
bag.
The whole affair was very sad
he was a plastic man
he was a plastic man

A plastic man will last forever
with a plastic mac
in the clement weather
of an indoor shopping superstore.
No, he never steps outside the door.
He's a lazy, hazy, instant gravy
polymer daisy plastic man
he's a plastic man

Plastic man loves to spend
on plastic goods that never end.
He's got a plastic car, a plastic life
a plastic lover and a plastic wife
he's a plastic man
he's a plastic man

Plastic love and Super Bowl,
does them both by remote control.
Loves to watch and eat the telly
loves to watch and eat the telly!?
believe me when you see his belly.
He's a rubbery, blubbery, not very cuddly
plastic man
he's a plastic man

Wrapped in rubber he loves to dance.
Sweats inside his plastic pants.
Whips it up into a trance
of Narcissism's withering glance
(in the mirror on the wall
the mirror there sees it all).
A polymer dream that's so inflated,
his love was popped – and laminated
he's a plastic man
he's a plastic man

You can bend him back but he won't break,
he's a plastic man make no mistake:
woodworm, mildew, dry-rot, rust,
have no fear of blue-eyed bugs,
impervious to wear and tear
this man could last for a thousand years!
But just for fun, everyday
he seems to get – thrown away
he's a plastic man
he's a plastic man

Now in years to come, as time goes by,
and archaeologists scratch the veneer of lies,
and everyone needs an oxygen pump,
(in paradise by the rubbish dump)
perhaps they'll wonder upon their knees
who did wrap each slice of cheese?
And say with awe across the land:

Verily it was the plastic man.

Rage!

Ahhhhhhhhhhhhhhhhhhhhhhhhhhhhhhhhhhhhhhhhhhhh-
hhhhhhhhhhhhhhhhhhhhhhhhhhhhhhhhhhhhhhhhhhhhhh-
hhhhhhhhhhhhhhhhhhhhhhhhhhhhhhhhhhhhhhhhhhhhhh-
hhhhhhhhhhhhhhhhhhhhhhhhhhhhhhhhhhhhhhhhhhhhhh-
hhhhhhhhhhhhhhhhhhhhhhhhhhhhhhhhhhhhhhhhhhhhh-
hhhhhhhhhhhhhhhhhhhhhhhhhhhhhhhhhhhhhhhhhhhhhh-
hhhhhhhhhhhhhhhhhhhhhhhhhhhhhhhhhhhhhhhhhhhhhh-
hhhhhhhhhhhhhhhhhhhhhhhhhhhhhhhhhhhhhhhhhhhhhh-
hhhhhhhhhhhhhhhhhhhhhhhhhhhhhhhhhhhhhhhhhhhhhh-
hhhhhhhhhhhhhhhhhhhhhhhhhhhhhhhhhhhhhhhhhhhhh-
hhhhhhhhhhhhhhhhhhhhhhhhhhhhhhhhhhhhhhhhhhhhh-
hhhhhhhhhhhhhhhhhhhhhhhhhhhhhhhhhhhhhhhhhhhhhh-
hhhhhhhhhhhhhhhhhhhhhhhhhhhhhhhhhhhhhhhhhhhhhh-
hhhhhhhhhhhhhhhhhhhhhhhhhhhhhhhhhhhhhhhhhhhhhh-
hhhhhhhhhhhhhhhhhhhhhh!

(It's a bit like a haiku, but with only one syllable.)

Wake Up!

Can I wake her with a kiss to the cheek?
Well she never moved her lips to speak.
Can I wake her by pulling the blind?
Her pale face lit but… showed no sign.

So, I tried to wake her with words of joy
singing like a stupid boy.
I tried to wake her with words of woe
like… all the poems that I know.

Well, if she heard them she never said
I read for years beside her bed.
Will she wake with an embrace so tight!?
I crushed her hands with all my might!

I began to wonder if she was ill,
I tried her with a pneumatic drill.
I began to wonder if she was dead.
I hit myself across the head
and told her that if she didn't wake up
I'd destroy myself…

I told her mankind would destroy itself
taking with it a host of amazing animals,
plants and insects which,
defying even our laws of science-fiction,
have evolved from what we call dead matter
into a rich profusion of intelligence
that would be lost forever.
If… she didn't wake up!

I also tried to tell her that unless she woke
I'd never know where she buried all that money
from the bank job.

I said: *Can I wake her*
for where she sank
all that money from the bank?

I was trying to wake her one more time
when across my face a light did shine.
So full of shock, no time to save,
I pushed her back – inside the grave.

I could hear the clamour of footsteps coming
and see the headlines of the Daily running:
Read all about it! Read all about it!
Poet tries to wake the dead
In quest for buried treasure chest!

I could not run,
my legs were lead.
I thrashed myself across the bed
and landed on the floor to see
that the one asleep was really me!

Can all the treasure of mother's wealth
be buried by my sleeping self?

The Smallest Cinema in the World

The wagon roaming freely in Regent's Park
is known as the smallest cinema in the world.
It contains a story
and is painted bright yellow just so you won't lose it.

It reminds me of the tortoise I had as a boy,
a hard dome
containing something quite exotic.
We called him Tank,
let him roam freely in the garden
and, just so we wouldn't lose him,
tied a bright yellow bucket on a length of bailer twine
through a little hole in the back of his shell.

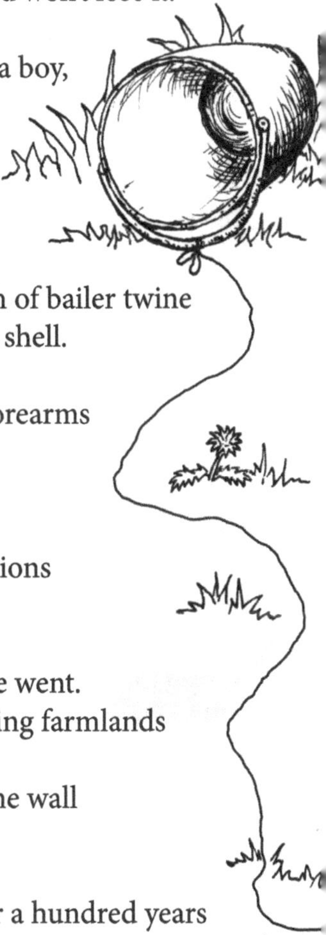

I can still see the tortoise's powerful forearms
pulling him forwards,
his long nails gripping the turf,
his Jurassic head jerking side to side,
his toothless jaws decapitating dandelions
and the bucket dragging behind him.

Tank dragged that bucket wherever he went.
It helped us find him in the surrounding farmlands
at the onset of winter.
When, he'd burrow beneath a dry stone wall
or into a mound of dying bracken.

My dad said tortoises can live for over a hundred years
but would probably die if left out during a cold winter.
A hundred years that's older than granny,
that's almost forever!

The thought gave me a warm feeling,
it made me happy for Tank.

Each year before the cold weather set in
we'd search for Tank's yellow bucket
follow the bailer twine through leaves
and dying undergrowth
and then, very carefully, we'd lift the sleeping Tank
into his box and put him in the loft.

A hundred years that's older than granny,
that's almost forever...
the only trouble was he'd still be here
when I had gone
and who'd look after him then?

One year we were late finding his bucket,
or slow to remember.
The first frosts had turned everything white.
Dad said if we bring him in now
it might be more of a shock to his system
than if we leave him out.
I was sick with guilt,
prayed for a mild winter
and before long his bucket disappeared under the snow.
I can't remember how he woke on that occasion.
Perhaps like Jesus he just re-appeared one day
(and at first we didn't recognise him
or thought he was the gardener).
I can remember him waking in the morning of other springs,
the anxiety uncovering the box,

the patterned shell, the dinosaur feet,
the relief on seeing his eyes blinking.
My mum would bathe his eyes with cotton wool
and I used to stroke his cool, dinosaur throat
with the back of my forefinger.
I liked that.
I like to think we both did.

I'd also like to think that's where the story ends
and the farmer carrying the yellow bucket
and puzzling over its contents:
the remains of Tank following his passage
through a combine harvester,
never really happened – as unreal as it looked –
an outtake from the film *The first 100 Years*
now showing at the smallest cinema in the world.

Tortoise in the Sky

Let us go then, you and I,
to feed the Tortoise in the Sky
like a patient grandpa sitting on a table;
let us go, through our secret garden gate
the little paths we make
where restless cats that cannot fly so well
hunt mistle thrushes breaking snail shells:
paths that follow far beyond the streets
and fields of troubled men
to lead you to an overwhelming Tortoise in the Sky…
Oh, do not ask, *What is it?*
let us go and make our visit.

Wordworms!

Words will sleep in the pages of books
entranced inside a nest of leaves.
They'll sleep, sometimes, for hundreds of years
waiting for you
to mouth and breathe their names.

Like grubs that sleep, dreaming of wings,
they curl up like the chrysalids
until one day a sudden breeze ruffles their nest…utters their names…

and muttering, spluttering out they slip…

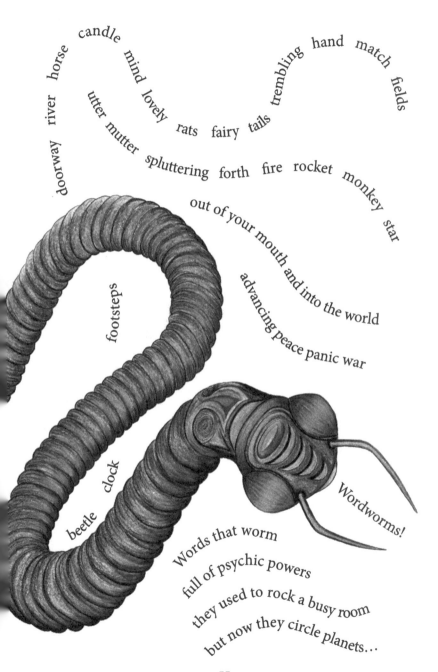

doorway river horse candle mind lovely rats fairy tails trembling hand match fields

utter mutter spluttering forth fire rocket monkey star

out of your mouth and into the world

advancing peace panic war

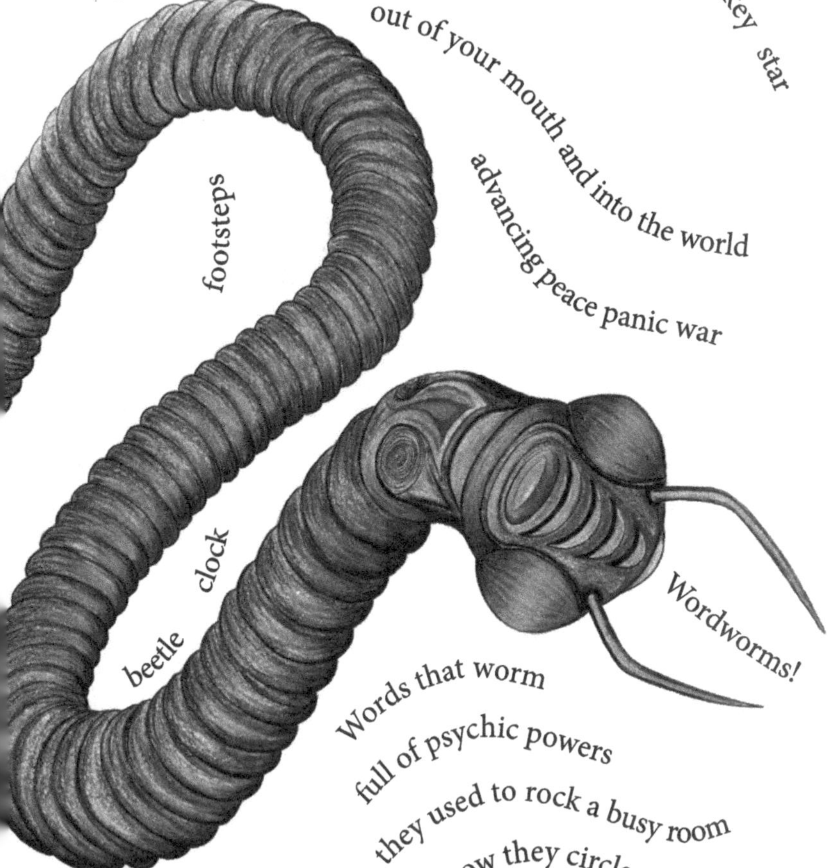

footsteps

clock

beetle

Wordworms!

Words that worm
full of psychic powers
they used to rock a busy room
but now they circle planets…

In liquid air
through silent rooms
they're chattering furiously
wordworms pass between these walls
in plagues we cannot see…

Invisible
when leaping
sylph-like in their speed
and only when they start to hatch
can their colours be perceived…

Beware the Babbleworm my son!
with the twenty heads and flickering tongues
the *Incoherum Babbleous* jabbering all at once:

with our interest free... bbchhh...
don't you love me anymore, Henry? Don't you remem...
bbchhh... *first thing I knew was smoke coming up*
through a crack in the floorboards...
bbchhh... *Hey sugar, wanna stop and dance?*

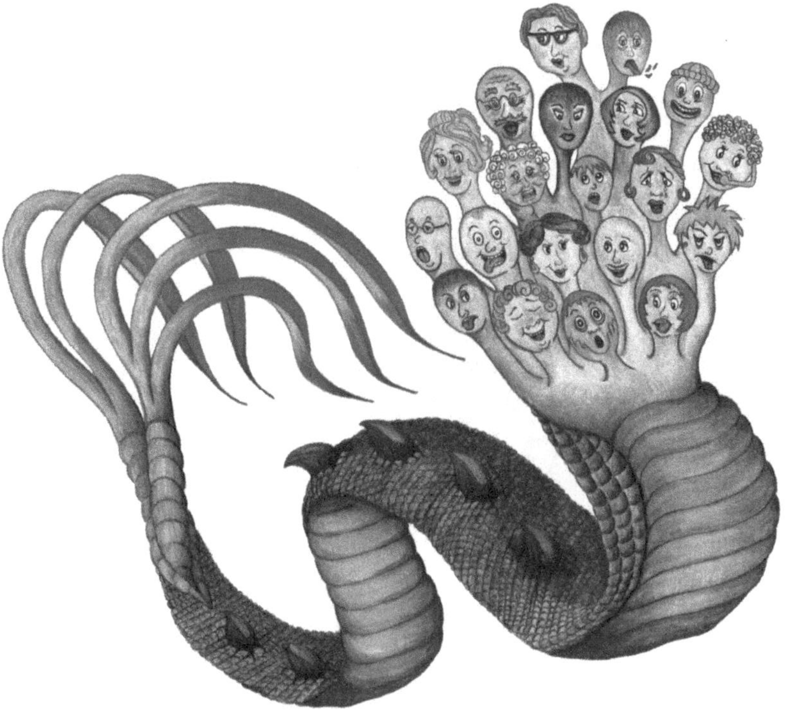

And you'll be undecided, in twenty minds at once...

Take care the Silver Sirenworm
the *Lusty Nymphadae*
a wriggling, giggling, glamourworm,
a nymph of olden times.
By her sweet mouth everyday words
whisper of blissful love
they'll put you under a powerful spell
and turn your faughts to thog.

Watch out! The endless Worrisome Worm!
The *Angst ad Infinitum*,
who never ceases gnawing
at the things that make you frightened.
Watch out! The endless Worrisome Worm!
Whose stomach knows no happy end
he'll eat you up
regurgitate
and eat you up, again.
Urrgh!

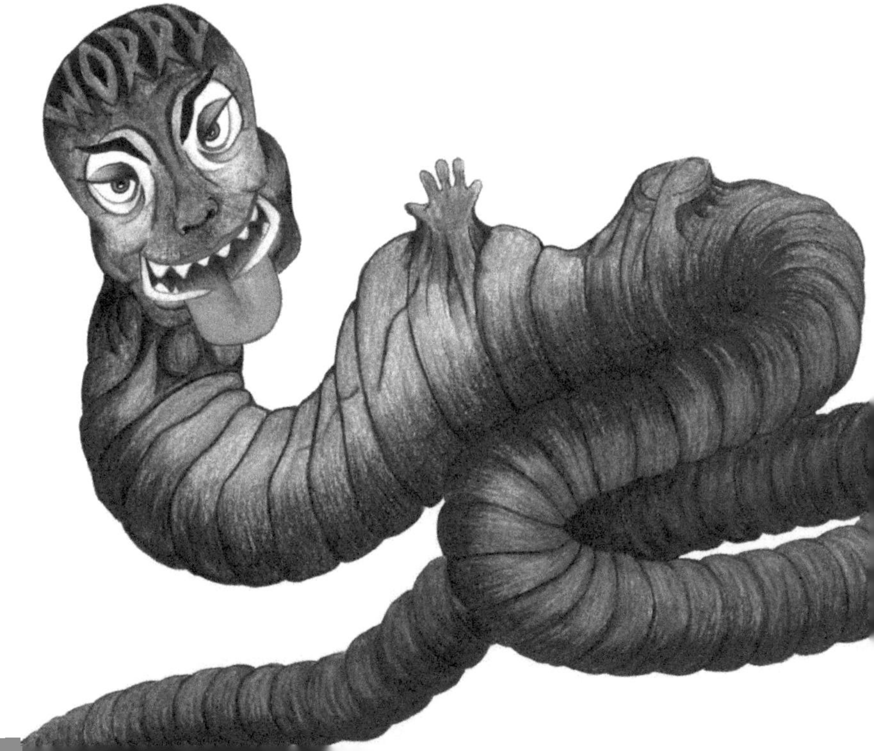

Whoa!
There are Wild Wordworms… *Mmh?*
Worms yet to be tamed… *A'haa!*
that live inside the jungle...
and scream aloud in pain.

Their cousins are the Tabooworms: *Explecio Vulgari* used as *effin'* sentence fillers by *Delinquent Juvenalli*.

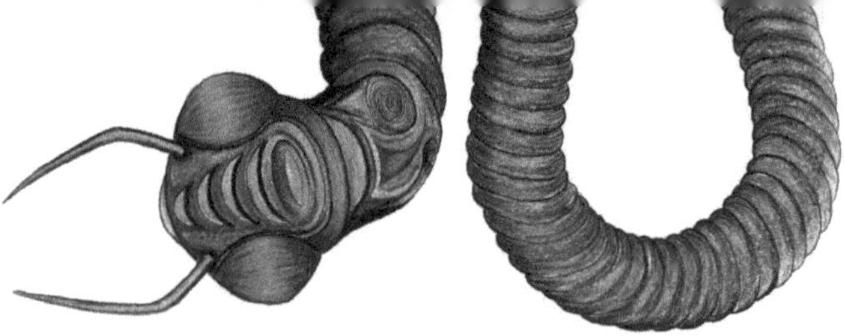

Some are gentle, some are tough.
Most are harmless sure enough
but those that voice something real
and change the way you think and feel
and on the street
begin to sing
what others only dare to think;
and singing breed a passionate swarm,
a frightening cloud that twists and turns,
and the humming grows till it makes you sweat,
and drives you from a sleepless bed
through the streets and to the market square
to find a thousand people gathered there,
in the right body, place and time
such wordworms will set a nation alive:
a new order unfolding its wings
from the husk of the old engulfed in flames!

Wordworms!
Words that worm
full of psychic powers
they used to rock a busy room
but now they circle planets…

Mark Gwynne Jones

Mark Gwynne Jones' life is a catalogue of near disasters. As a boy he was trapped in a burning van, crashed through the ice of a frozen lake, was swept out to sea in the Mediterranean and, like a fool, allowed his brother to shoot bottles off the top of his head. Sadly, Mark survived and went on to write quite a lot of poetry. Some of which is in this book.

www.markgwynnejones.wordpress.com
www.route-online.com